PIONEERS

of the

AIR

BY

MOLLY BU...

13 MAY 2013 Tynnwyd o'r stoc

- 6 JUL 2013 Withdrawn

CAERPHILLY
COUNTY BOROUGH COUNCIL
CYNGOR BWRDEISTREF SIROL
CAERFFILI

SCHOOLS LIBRARY SERVICE

Please return / renew this item by the last date shown above
Dychwelwch / Adnewyddwch erbyn y dyddiad olaf y nodir yma

D0727267

The Dream of Flight

THE MODERN AIR TRAVELLER

Today the modern traveller can feel comfortable in the knowledge that the plane they board will take them to their planned destination, along a known route and constantly in touch with the rest of the world. For the early pioneers it was a flight into the unknown. They were flying in untested craft, with little means of navigation, unsure if they would live to see where they had landed.

Most people today take flying, air travel and speed for granted. It is difficult to imagine the bravery, inventiveness and sometimes sheer genius of the first flying pioneers. Every challenge and every achievement was greeted with incredulity and public acclaim, from the first balloon flight in 1783, to the first successful piloted flight by the Wright brothers in 1903. Flying like the birds was a dream. When people fantasized about flying to America or sending a man to the moon, they never thought that both would become a reality.

In the early years, many attempts were made to imitate birds but the 19th century saw two developments that formed the basis of flying and aircraft – the science of flight and the emergence of people who were prepared to experiment with, make, develop, test and pilot the first flying machines. These were the pioneers of the air.

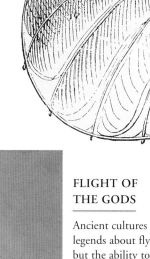

FLIGHT OF THE GODS

Ancient cultures had legends about flying, but the ability to do so was generally reserved for the gods. In Greek mythology, Daedalus and his son Icarus built wings to allow them to fly. However, ignoring his father's warnings, Icarus flew too near the sun and the wax that held the feathers together melted and he fell to his death.

ART & AERONAUTICS

The 15th-century artist, Leonardo da Vinci, showed a remarkable knowledge of aeronautics way before his time. He studied birds in flight and made sketches of a man-powered flying machine as early as 1500. This model of his flapping-wing machine shows that Leonardo was unable to unlock the secret of enabling man to fly – it would have required super-human stamina and endurance to keep the craft in the air.

THE BIRDMEN

There are over 50 documented instances of people trying to fly before 1880. Le Besnier (below) was a French locksmith who was reported to have 'flown' several feet with the aid of a pair of wood and tafetta wings. The Englishman Thomas Pelling became a local celebrity as a birdman, but he met an untimely end when he jumped from a church tower: the rope broke and he fell to his death. Viennese watchmaker Jacob Degen (left) devised one of the more bizarre early flying machines in approximately 1811. His flapping-wing aircraft, or *ornithopter,* had two flaps that were fastened to his back by a yoke. He moved them up and down with levers worked by his hands and feet. It is not known how far the machine took him, if indeed it ever got off the ground!

PIONEERS OF THE AIR
-A Time Line-

~1500~
Leonardo da Vinci sketches early designs for man-powered flying machines

~1783~
First hot-air balloon flight in a Montgolfier balloon

First hydrogen balloon flight by Professor Jacques Charles

~1809~
George Cayley's first successful glider flight

~1843~
Cayley designs early helicopter

~1867~
Wilbur Wright born

~1871~
Orville Wright born

~1884~
Charles Renard and Arthur Krebs fly first controllable and powered airship, La France

~1887~
Lawrence Hargrave invents rotary engine

~1893~
Hargrave develops box kite

Up, Up & Away

The 17th and 18th centuries also saw some highly impractical schemes to get airborne. In 1670 Francesco de Lana, a Jesuit priest, suggested a design for an aerial ship suspended by four copper spheres emptied of air. Unfortunately, he overlooked the fact that the atmospheric pressure would have collapsed the spheres.

By the late 1700s, it was well known that objects that were lighter than air would rise, but the real pioneers of this knowledge were the brothers Joseph and Etienne Montgolfier. Working in their father's paper factory in south-east France, they noticed how paper would be lifted up the chimney when it was put on the fire. They started to experiment and became convinced that a large bag filled with hot air would rise. The two brothers burned a mixture of wool and straw which produced what they thought was a 'new' gas. After conducting trials with models, they built a large linen bag covered with stiff paper and fastened with buttons, creating the first hot-air balloon. The Montgolfier brothers refused to believe it was just hot air that made their balloon rise, and not their 'Montgolfier gas'. Nevertheless, it was due to them that the first human being, Jean François Pilâtre de Rosier, rose from the ground in a tethered balloon.

FLYING HIGH

The first living creatures to fly in free flight were three animals; a sheep, a duck and a cockerel. They flew in a wicker basket suspended from a balloon on 19 September 1783; a balloon designed by the Montgolfier brothers.

MONTGOLFIER ASCENT

On 21 November 1783, before an amazed Parisian crowd, Jean François Pilâtre de Rosier, accompanied by the Marquis d'Arlandes, took off in a Montgolfier balloon. They flew in free flight over the city for 23 minutes, landing 16 kilometres (10 miles) away. This flight is acknowledged as the first time a man actually flew.

BALLOONS IN WARFARE

One of the more practical uses of balloons was in warfare. Thaddeus Lowe constructed four balloons for the Union Army in Virginia in 1862. They were used during the American Civil War for observation purposes.

JACQUES CHARLES
(1746-1823)

As the Montgolfier brothers were testing their balloon, the French physicist Professor Jacques Charles was building a balloon of varnished silk which he filled with hydrogen, known to be 14 times lighter than air. The unmanned balloon was released in Paris in August 1783, rose into the air and was carried 24 kilometres (15 miles) to the village of Gonesse. The peasants thought they were being attacked by a monster from the sky and destroyed the balloon with sticks and pitchforks. Charles had better luck with his next hydrogen-filled balloon. Accompanied by his assistant Nicolas Robert, the *Charlière* (as hydrogen balloons became known) set off from the Tuileries Gardens in Paris watched by a crowd of 200,000 people. It travelled 46.5 kilometres (29 miles).

BALLOON RACES

Ballooning developed quickly, following the success of the Montgolfier brothers. Balloon racing became a popular sport with the development of the hydrogen-filled balloon, as can be seen here in Germany in 1908. But ballooning had its limitations – steering was completely dependent on the direction of the wind and the material used was flammable and susceptible to punctures.

Early Aircraft

ALBERTO SANTOS-DUMONT

Ballooning was popular in the 1800s, but others were turning their attention to controllable flight. The major problem for lighter-than-air craft was the failure to find a lightweight source of power. In August 1884 Charles Renard and Arthur Krebs, officers of the French Corps of Engineers, flew the first controllable and powered airship (or dirigible as airships were then known). Others were looking to develop heavier-than-air craft, and it was the kite, first flown by the Chinese over 2,000 years ago, that became the inspiration for many inventors. Sir George Cayley used the idea of a kite to discover the basic aeronautical principles. He built the first successful aeroplane, admittedly a model glider, but it actually flew! It fell to an Australian, Lawrence Hargrave, to build the box kite that was the key to successful flight and aeronautical design.

In 1852, a small steam engine was fitted to a sausage-shaped balloon and the airship was created. In 1901, the colourful Brazilian Alberto Santos-Dumont flew his airship around the Eiffel Tower in Paris, causing much excitement amongst the crowds. It was a feat which won him the first prize ever given for aerial achievement. Santos-Dumont used his airships like taxis, often dropping in on friends, leaving his airship tied to their house. He went on to build a box kite bi-plane in which he made the first officially observed flight in Europe in 1906. Santos-Dumont was very popular with the French people, not so much for his flying successes as for his many crashes.

OTTO LILIENTHAL (1849-96)

The German Otto Lilienthal was the first to build and fly a glider capable of carrying a person. Lilienthal made more than 2,500 flights, gradually improving his design until he was gliding almost half a kilometre (a quarter of a mile). He relied on the movement of his body to control the aircraft but in 1896 he lost control and the glider crashed, killing him. His last words were '*sacrifices must be made*', reflecting the true spirit of these early pioneers.

SIR GEORGE CAYLEY (1773-1857)

Sir George Cayley is credited with several scientific principles and inventions, but it is in the field of aeronautics that he made his mark. Known as both 'The Father of Aerial Navigation' and 'The Father of Flight', Cayley had a huge influence on the development of flight as he recognized the necessity of a scientific approach. In 1804 he built a glider that was strong enough to carry his gardener boy several feet. A later, stronger, model carried his coachman across a narrow valley. On landing, the coachman immediately handed Cayley his notice!

AERIAL STEAM CARRIAGE

English engineer William Samuel Henson was a great admirer of George Cayley's work and studied his principles. In 1842, he filed a patent for the Aerial Steam Carriage – the first design for a completely mechanically powered aircraft that actually looked like an aeroplane. It had two propellers that were driven by a steam engine. A model was built in 1847 but the weight of the engine forced the plane to glide downwards.

LANGLEY'S AERODROME

Dr Samuel Pierpont Langley was a highly-respected American scientist who designed several tandem-winged planes, one of which was steam driven. He received a government grant to make a full-sized aircraft called the Aerodrome, which was petrol driven. The first piloted test flight was in 1903 when it was launched by catapult from the roof of a houseboat on the Potomac River. The launching mechanism failed and the plane plunged into the river, nearly drowning the pilot. Disappointed and out of funds, Langley gave up the challenge to fly.

THE BOX KITE

Lawrence Hargrave (1850-1915) had little scientific knowledge but he was a good engineer. He invented the rotary engine in 1887 but it is his invention of the box kite in 1893 that established his place in aviation history. Hargrave demonstrated the lifting power of his box kite when he suspended himself below four kites strung together. He was lifted 5 metres (16 feet) into the air. By 1906, most of the first aeroplanes developed in Europe were designed with wings based on Hargrave's box kite design.

THE FIRST FLIGHT

Only five people were witness to the world's first powered flight. The scene was set on sand dunes outside Kitty Hawk in North Carolina, USA. This peninsula was chosen because of the strong, almost continuous winds. Wilbur had to run alongside, holding the wing of the *Flyer* to balance it on the track. Then Orville took off on his historic flight. The flight lasted 12 seconds and covered a distance of 37 metres (120 feet). This is less than the wingspan of a modern airliner, but at the time it represented a new age in technology.

ACHIEVING RECOGNITION

Initially, Orville and Wilbur Wright received very little recognition for their success from their own countrymen. For several years after the first flight, people were sceptical about their achievement. Wilbur went to France to demonstrate a later model of their famous *Flyer*. On 8 October 1908, he was ready for his first flight. A large crowd gathered to watch, many expecting the test to be a failure. When Wilbur successfully landed, the crowd went mad with excitement. The next day, all the French newspapers wrote of his achievement.

THE BICYCLE MEN

Orville (1871–1948), left, and Wilbur (1867–1912) Wright were keen experimenters and skilled craftsmen. They were able to think about a machine's requirements, make it and watch it work! They owned a business manufacturing and repairing bicycles. They were both private men who were diligent and determined, and they deserved their success. The value of their contribution to flying, besides being the first to fly in a heavier-than-air machine, was the way they proved the value of a scientific approach rather than the 'build it and see' attitude that had prevailed.

The Wright Brothers

The excitement and interest in flight was growing to almost fever pitch at the turn of the 20th century. Both airships and other lighter-than-air machines were flying successfully. Lots of publicity was focused on the engineers and scientists trying to develop the first powered and controllable aeroplane capable of carrying a man. When the first successful flight was made, it was by someone who had not been in the public eye. It all began in 1878 when two young brothers, Orville and Wilbur Wright, were given a toy helicopter. This, and reading the work of Otto Lilienthal, spurred them to actively experiment with flying machines. They succeeded in building and piloting one of the largest gliders ever built. They built their own wind tunnel to aid their experiments, and also built a small 12-horsepower petrol engine to power the craft.

Then, on 17 December 1903, they travelled with their newly designed plane, *Flyer*, to the Kill Devil Hill sand dunes at Kitty Hawk. The rest is history.

BODYWORK

This model shows how Orville operated the controls of the *Flyer*. He had to lie face down on the lower wing, left of centre to counterbalance the weight of the engine. He operated the elevator control lever with his hand and other controls with his hips.

TELEGRAM!

The Wright brothers made four successful flights, at Kitty Hawk. Orville sent a telegram to their father announcing their victory and asked him to inform the press. Remarkably the press reaction was luke-warm, not helped by the fact that the telegraph operator had mistakenly put that the duration of the flight was 57 seconds. The real time of 12 seconds seemed anti-climactic.

SUCCESS AND FAILURE

At first, the US Government didn't acknowledge the Wright Brothers' claims that they could fly. While Wilbur was flying in France, Orville was breaking records for endurance in America. Then, on 17 September 1908, mechanical failure caused the *Flyer* to crash. Orville broke his leg, but his passenger, Lieutenant Selfridge, was killed making him the first victim of an aeroplane disaster. Not to be deterred, Orville carried on and enjoyed success the following year in Berlin as can be seen here.

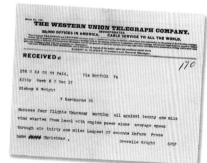

LOUIS BLÉRIOT
& FAMILY

Those Magnificent Men & their Flying Machines

The first decade of the 20th century saw flying becoming established. The Wright brothers had set the scene and many others wanted to follow. In America, Glenn Curtiss and his associates were actively involved in the Aerial Experiment Association. In France, the Voissin brothers adapted their factory to build aeroplanes, and enthusiasts followed every development with excitement. Even Santos-Dumont transferred his interest from airships to aircraft, much to the delight of the French crowds as his 'near misses' became even more dramatic. But there were people who mistrusted the idea of flight, and others who discouraged it. In England in 1909, A.V. Roe flew his tri-plane and was threatened with prosecution for disturbing the peace, but a few days later this was forgotten when the Frenchman Louis Blériot successfully flew across the English Channel. This flight was one of the most important advances in aviation.

Louis Blériot (1872-1936) had made a fortune and spent most of it on flying. He had a reputation for being enthusiastic about crazy ideas and was seen as a bit of a joke. He bought several aeroplanes from the Voissin brothers and the kindest that can be said of their designs is that many of them were misguided. On one occasion, in a demonstration in Paris, a Voissin aeroplane fell apart before take off! But the result of Blériot's cross-Channel flight was remarkable. Blériot amassed another fortune selling hundreds of his planes, but sadly his flying skills did not improve. After a crash he had to give up flying and he died virtually penniless in 1936.

CROSSING THE ENGLISH CHANNEL

At the beginning of 1909, the London *Daily Mail* offered a £1,000 prize to anyone who could fly across the Channel. Many tried, including two serious challengers; Count Charles de Lambert, who withdrew after crashing, and Hubert Latham, whose engine failed several miles out to sea, where he sat, smoking a cigar, waiting to be rescued. The disorganized Blériot won the prize on 25 July 1909, when he set off from France in poor visibility with no compass. Finding that he was lost, he followed some fishing boats, guessing they were heading for Dover. When he reached England, he flew along the coastline until he saw a man waving a flag. He crash-landed 37 minutes after leaving France, becoming an instant celebrity.

Le Petit Journal

LA TRAVERSÉE DU PAS-DE-CALAIS EN AÉROPLANE
Blériot atterrit sur la falaise de Douvres

GLENN CURTISS (1878-1930)

Curtiss was an American pioneer who conducted similar research to the Wright brothers, although he placed his pilots in a sitting position. He made his first public flight in the USA on 12 March 1908, and in 1909, won the world's first air race in Rheims, France. Local wine growers had organized a Festival of Flying, and there was prize money and trophies to be won. Curtiss won the most prestigious: the Gordon Bennett Cup.

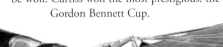

THE DEPERDUSSIN

By 1913, French aviation led the world. The Deperdussin was difficult to fly but could reach speeds in excess of 160 kilometres (100 miles) an hour – the fastest thing in the sky. For more practical use, the seaplane was also being developed, like this Deperdussin Seagull.

TOM SOPWITH (1888-1989)

Tom Sopwith made a memorable debut on the aeronautical scene in 1910 when he crashed his plane at Brooklands in an early British air display. The next day he decided to learn to fly! He became a test pilot; set up a flying school; and designed and manufactured many of the aircraft used in the First World War.

SAMUEL CODY (1862-1913)

Samuel Franklin Cody was a larger-than-life character who, in 1908, made the first flight in England. He demonstrated the abilities of man-carrying kites with the help of his family – on one occasion he lifted his wife aloft in a kite and forgot her for several hours! Later, Cody turned his attention to manned flight. The aircraft he built reflected Cody's character. They were so large they were known as 'Flying Cathedrals'.

Race for the Skies

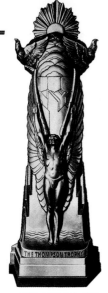

US AIR RACES

By the 1930s, air races were attracting huge crowds in the United States. The premier race was for the Thompson Trophy. It was open to all aircraft over a course of 80.5 kilometres (50 miles). The first all-women race took place in Cleveland in 1929 and it became known as the 'Powder-puff Derby'. It had 23 competitors, including Amelia Earhart. But other women had already made their mark in aviation history. The French Baroness de Laroche was the first woman to receive a pilot's licence by the Aéro Club of France in 1910.

The interest in flight had been growing steadily, but Blériot's cross-Channel flight in 1909 caused an unparalleled surge of excitement. The Festival of Flying in Rheims was attended by royalty and people travelled from all over the world to be there. It became an annual event. There were many other awards and prizes, events and exhibitions which gave a great boost to the development of the aeroplane. The Aéro Club of America sponsored events. Prize money was offered for a 'Round Britain' flight. The air races for the Lockheed, Pullitzer and Thompson trophies still take place in the US today. But the most prized in these early days was the Schneider Trophy. It is considered that the races for the Schneider Trophy accelerated progress so much that twenty years of research were condensed into just six. Race winners became heroes.

AIR SHOWS

After the First World War, many unemployed pilots found work as travelling showmen, entertaining the crowds with aerial tricks such as wing walking. A combined air and car display took place at Brooklands Circuit in England. The Circuit had been built for car racing, but failed to attract good audiences. The central grassed area was used to introduce aviation as an additional attraction.

JIMMY DOOLITTLE

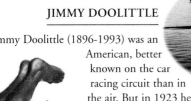

Jimmy Doolittle (1896-1993) was an American, better known on the car racing circuit than in the air. But in 1923 he won the Schneider Trophy in a US Army seaplane (above). He went on to win the first Bendix Trophy, and the Thompson Trophy, where he set a new world record speed of 473 kilometres (294 miles) per hour. He also pioneered the use of aeronautical instruments and was the first man to fly 'blind' in 1929, guided purely by instruments.

THE SCHNEIDER TROPHY

Jacques Schneider presented this bronze trophy to the Aéro Club of France in 1913. It was originally meant to encourage marine craft but it developed into an air race. The first race was in Monaco in 1913, but was suspended during the First World War and restarted in 1919 off the Isle of Wight. Races continued until 1931 when Britain won the trophy outright, having won three consecutive races.

AVIATION MEETS

Aviation meetings were very popular and gave people the opportunity to get close to aeroplanes. Huge crowds attended most of the air displays.

WINNING THE SCHNEIDER TROPHY

The first winner of the Schneider trophy was Maurice Prevost. He was the only pilot to complete the course. Tom Sopwith and Harry Hawker brought a Sopwith Tabloid aeroplane for the 1914 race. It won at an average speed of 139.5 kilometres (86.7 miles) per hour, almost double that of the previous year's winner. The last race of 1931 was won by a Supermarine S 6B at an average speed of 547 kilometres (340 miles) per hour.
Like this replica, the high-speed Schneider floatplanes provided the opportunities for developing strong, light, streamlined machines, which pointed the way to the fighters of the future.

PIONEERS OF THE AIR
-A TIME LINE-

~1909~
First aviation exhibition is sponsored by the City of Rheims

Glenn Curtiss wins world's first air race

~1910~
Baroness Raymonde de Laroche becomes the first woman to gain her pilot's licence

~1913~
First race takes place for the Schneider Trophy

~1914-18~
First World War produces many flying aces and accelerates developments in aviation

~1917~
William Boeing starts The Boeing Airplane Company

~1919~
Alcock and Brown fly non-stop across the Atlantic

~1922~
Juan Trippe starts Colonial Air Transport, the forerunner to Pan Am

~1924~
Alan Cobham flies from London to Cape Town

The First World War

COUNT ZEPPELIN

This commemorative medal is of Count Ferdinand von Zeppelin, the founder of the company which built the first fleet of Zeppelin airships. They were 128 metres (420 feet) long with a basic design of 16 internal gas cells encased in a shell of aluminium and cotton.

They were the largest machines ever to have flown. Before the war they were used to carry passengers, setting up the first passenger air service. During the war they were used as bombers.

Few people believed that there was any value to aircraft in wartime, except for reconnaissance. There were some half-hearted experiments at dropping bombs and torpedoes and firing guns from planes but they weren't taken seriously. When the first allied planes flew out to France in 1914, they didn't carry guns. Their only instructions were to ram any Zeppelin airship they came across. The Germans had the advantage in the air in the first two years of the war. They used aeroplanes designed by a young Dutchman, Anthony Fokker. His designs were original and purposeful, and early on in the war, he designed an interruptor gear which allowed a forward-facing gun to be fired through propellers without damaging them. By 1916 the allies, too, were developing aeroplanes as war machines. A different kind of flying was required. The newly trained pilots of the First World War were the pioneers of their time; the aces of the air.

LA PUIS.

AMERICA'S ACE

Captain Eddie Rickenbacker was America's most celebrated hero of the First World War. Before the war, he was a top racing car driver. When the Americans joined the war in April 1917, Rickenbacker was originally rejected as a pilot because at the age of 27 he was considered too old. He finally managed to join a squadron, but as Colonel Billy Mitchell's driver. It was Colonel Mitchell who arranged for Rickenbacker's pilot training. By the end of the war, Rickenbacker had shot down four balloons and 22 aircraft to become America's top flying ace.

MILITAIRE
LA FRANCE

THE ALLIED ATTACKS

The British developed a strategy for combating the German's early superiority in the skies. It was to improve aircraft, to train personnel and to take the air war to the Germans – attacking and pursuing them relentlessly. Factories were built, aircraft design and construction became an established business and planes were rapidly developed. The French supported these plans and many allied aces made their mark: René Fonck from France, Edward (Micky) Mannock from Britain and William (Billy) Bishop from Canada, to name but a few.

THE FOKKER EINDECKER

Anthony Fokker (1890-1939) had two interests in life, aeroplanes and money. He admitted that he would sell anything to the first who showed him the money. The British were not interested in Fokker's designs. It was the Germans who took the initiative and the Fokker Eindecker was in use from the first days of the war. After the war, Fokker returned to his native Holland and started his own factory. He was a pioneer of aircraft design developing a series of high-winged monoplanes.

THE RED BARON

Baron Manfred von Richthofen (1882-1918) was a popular hero in Germany. His distinctive red Fokker tri-plane earned him the nickname 'The Red Baron'. He received the highest German honour for his service, the Ordre pour le Merité, which became known as the Blue Max after Max Immelmann, another flying ace and recipient of the award. Richthofen was credited with shooting down 80 allied planes during the First World War before he himself was shot down and killed.

Record Breakers

At the end of the First World War there were many unwanted, cheap aircraft available producing a situation that was right for development, adventure and innovation. Races such as the Schneider Trophy were resumed after the war and now there were plenty of trained pilots (both men and women) to challenge existing records. Aviators saw opportunities for establishing new records in every corner of the world. The 1920s and 1930s saw new airways opened, and slowly and steadily the world grew smaller. Media interest was at its height and the excitement generated by these record breakers and pioneers spread worldwide.

THE DARLING OF THE PEOPLE

In 1928, the Australian Bert Hinkler flew from London to Darwin, prompting a young working-class British woman to vow to do the same. Amy Johnson (1903-1941) and her fisherman father scraped together enough money to purchase a Gypsy Moth. Johnson achieved her aim in 1930, and although she took four days longer than Hinkler, she was the first woman to fly the route solo and she became the 'darling of the people'. Crowds flocked to see her, and songs and poems were written about her.

THE DE HAVILLAND GYPSY MOTH

The de Havilland Gypsy Moth was Britain's most popular light aircraft. Amy Johnson named hers 'Jason' and painted it dark green, her lucky colour. Her Moth was considered far too small for the journey she had in mind, but remarkably the plane made it intact.

ALCOCK AND BROWN

Captain John Alcock and Lieutenant Arthur Whitten-Brown were the first to fly non-stop across the Atlantic on 14 June 1919. It proved to be an epic journey. They took off from Newfoundland and, almost straight away, their problems began. The radio failed; their specially heated suits were not working; and a section of exhaust fell off. When they hit bad weather, Alcock took the plane high to avoid snow clouds. The engines began to get blocked by ice, so Brown had to clamber along the wing and chip the ice away with a knife several times. They were greatly relieved when they finally landed in Ireland (unfortunately in a bog), 16 hours after take-off. A statue stands at Heathrow Airport, honouring their achievement.

28

THE FIRST SOLO ATLANTIC CROSSING

Charles Lindbergh took off from Roosevelt Field in New York on 20 May 1927. He was unprepared for the journey, but when he heard that the weather conditions were going to be good, he seized the opportunity. There to see him take off was Anthony Fokker, who was so convinced that Lindbergh would not make it over the trees, let alone across the Atlantic, he went to the end of the runway to help with the rescue. But the greatest difficulty Lindbergh faced was staying awake; he had to keep opening the side window and pinching himself. He landed in Paris 33½ hours later. He was the 92nd person to cross the Atlantic by air, but the first to fly solo. He became instantly famous.

CHARLES LINDBERGH (1902-74)

Charles Lindbergh was probably the most famous aviator of his time. He began his flying career delivering the mail. When the Orteig prize of $25,000 was announced for the first person to cross the Atlantic, Lindbergh decided to enter. He had difficulty obtaining a plane as the main manufacturers would not risk a plane on an unknown pilot. With the help of some businessmen, he approached Ryan Aircraft who agreed to modify their single-engine M62 to his specification. In return for their help, the businessmen had one request, that he name the plane after their city. He called it *The Spirit of St Louis*. The plane was built in two months at a cost of $6,000.

POLE TO POLE

Polar exploration and aviation were seen as the big adventures of the age. The Norwegian Raoul Amundsen was the first man to reach the South Pole on foot and then wanted to conquer the North Pole. He did so in an airship, which had been built by the Italian Umberto Nobile in 1928.

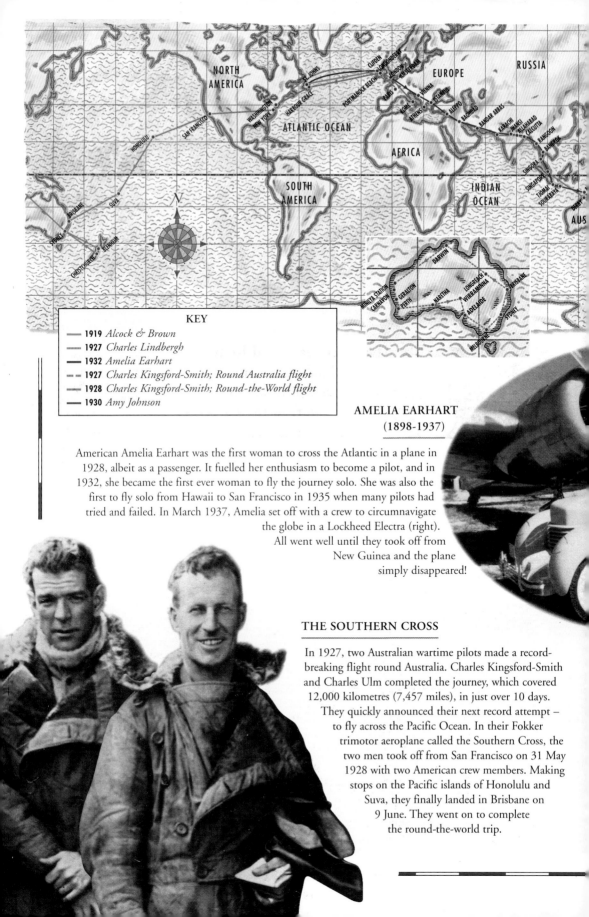

NORTH
AMERICA

RUSSIA

EUROPE

CLIFDEN
LONDONDERRY
ST JOHNS
LONDON
MARSEILLES
WASHINGTON
PORTMARNOCK BEACH
VIENNA
ISTANBUL
NEW YORK
PARIS
HARBOUR GRACE
ALEPPO
ROME
ATHENS
BAGHDAD
BANDAR ABBAS
SAN FRANCISCO
KARACHI
JHANSI
ALLAHABAD
HONOLULU
CALCUTTA
RANGOON

ATLANTIC OCEAN

AFRICA

BANGKOK

SINGORA
SINGAPORE

SOUTH
AMERICA

INDIAN
OCEAN

TJOMAL
SOURABAYA

DERBY
AUS

BRISBANE
SUVA

SYDNEY
BLENHEIM

CHRISTCHURCH

DARWIN

MUNLYA STATION
CARNARVON
GERALTON
PERTH
MARETHA
LONGREACH
WINRAMINNA
ADELAIDE
BRISBANE
SYDNET

MELBOURNE

KEY

—— **1919** *Alcock & Brown*
—— **1927** *Charles Lindbergh*
—— **1932** *Amelia Earhart*
-- -- **1927** *Charles Kingsford-Smith; Round Australia flight*
—·—· **1928** *Charles Kingsford-Smith; Round-the-World flight*
—— **1930** *Amy Johnson*

AMELIA EARHART
(1898-1937)

American Amelia Earhart was the first woman to cross the Atlantic in a plane in 1928, albeit as a passenger. It fuelled her enthusiasm to become a pilot, and in 1932, she became the first ever woman to fly the journey solo. She was also the first to fly solo from Hawaii to San Francisco in 1935 when many pilots had tried and failed. In March 1937, Amelia set off with a crew to circumnavigate the globe in a Lockheed Electra (right). All went well until they took off from New Guinea and the plane simply disappeared!

THE SOUTHERN CROSS

In 1927, two Australian wartime pilots made a record-breaking flight round Australia. Charles Kingsford-Smith and Charles Ulm completed the journey, which covered 12,000 kilometres (7,457 miles), in just over 10 days. They quickly announced their next record attempt – to fly across the Pacific Ocean. In their Fokker trimotor aeroplane called the Southern Cross, the two men took off from San Francisco on 31 May 1928 with two American crew members. Making stops on the Pacific islands of Honolulu and Suva, they finally landed in Brisbane on 9 June. They went on to complete the round-the-world trip.

Record Breakers

The race for the pioneers was not only to reach new countries. By the 1930s they were also competing to fly the farthest, the fastest, the highest and to stay the longest in the air. In 1932, Professor Auguste Piccard took his hot-air balloon to a height of 17,000 metres (56,000 feet) but, as with other records, it was soon broken. The following year a Russian high-altitude balloon reached 19,000 metres (62,300 feet). Wiley Post and Harold Getty set a record in 1931 for circling the globe in a Lockheed Vega in just eight and half days. McCready and Kelly established an endurance record by staying aloft in their Fokker monoplane for 38 hours. And the speed records were being smashed continually at the many air races.

FLYING HIGH

Auguste Piccard, seen here celebrating his 49th birthday with a topical cake, held the high-altitude record in 1932. This was a great achievement as there were no modern safeguards on board his balloon. There was a huge risk of physical injury as his capsule was not pressurized, as modern aircraft are today. The higher one flies, the lower the air density and pressure, and so he was risking burst blood vessels, burst ear drums, and even blackouts.

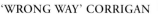

'WRONG WAY' CORRIGAN

Douglas Corrigan was a mechanic who had once shaken hands with Lindbergh, and ever since had been determined to follow in his footsteps, or rather his air route. The problem was he had neither plane nor the means to obtain one. He bought a Curtiss Robin for $300 and worked at repairing and improving it. He attached most of the electronic instruments on to the panel with tape and wire, and fitted fuel tanks on the front of his plane which meant he couldn't clearly see where he was going. When he applied for a licence to cross the Atlantic, unsurprisingly he was refused. He wished the inspector a 'bon voyage' and flew off, claiming he was returning home. An hour later he was spotted crossing the Atlantic. He landed in Ireland the next day, saying his compass had malfunctioned and so he'd gone the wrong way. Wrong Way Corrigan, as he became known, received a ticker-tape reception when he returned home to New York, and was made an honorary member of the Liars Club.

Only Pan American flies to all 6 continents!

World's most experienced airline

PAN AMERICAN WORLD AIRWAYS

Commercial Flight

O nce the pioneers had opened up the air routes, commercial aviation developed swiftly. Carrying mail was one of the first commercial uses for aircraft, and it wasn't long before passenger flights were on the increase. In 1937, Imperial Airways inaugurated the first commercial air service across the Atlantic with two Short 'C' Class flying boats. Flying boats were used when destinations were near suitable stretches of water thus saving the cost of building expensive airfields. The pioneers of commercial flight were not only the pilots, they included the designers, engineers and those who understood the science of flight.

PAN AMERICAN AIRWAYS

Pan American World Airways was started by businessman Juan Trippe in 1922. He was not particularly interested in aviation but, like others around the world, he recognized the future role of the aeroplane. Trippe was constantly looking to improve his planes and his service. Pan Am was one of the first operators to order a jetliner in 1953 – the Boeing 707-120.

THE DC2/3

In the stick-and-string days of the past, aeroplanes were often designed and built in a few weeks. If they didn't work, they were pulled to pieces, redesigned and rebuilt. But the new airlines demanded bigger and better aircraft to suit the needs of the increasing number of travellers. Manufacturing firms, like Douglas and Boeing, began to build passenger craft, and the Douglas DC2/3 became the leading airliner for the next 20 years.

AIRSHIP TRAVEL

The 1920s and 30s were golden eras for airships, the two most famous being the *Graf Zeppelin* and the *Hindenburg*. They carried thousands of passengers across the Atlantic for several years. Then, in 1937, the *Hindenburg* set off from Berlin en route to the United States. As it came in to land, there was an explosion and the whole ship quickly went up in flames. Incredibly, 61 of the 97 passengers survived, but people lost confidence, bringing the airship era to an abrupt end.

2 TAGEN NACH NORD-AMERIKA! DEUTSCHE ZEPPELIN-REEDEREI

THE AERODROME

The aircraft was not always first choice for travel in the 1930s. One of the problems was the placing of airfields. It often took longer to get to and from the aerodrome than the flight itself, and other forms of transport, like the train, ship and car, were also developing. Berlin airport shown here in 1937, was one of the first purpose built. Croydon airport was one of the biggest and by 1939 Imperial Airways was offering services to far-away destinations such as Karachi, Cape Town, Lake Victoria, Singapore and Brisbane.

THE MAIL MAN

The first mail flights were between New York and Chicago in surplus war planes bought by the US post office. In the first year, 18 pilots were killed and fears grew that the service would be closed down. In 1921, to demonstrate its value, a cross-country flight from San Francisco to New York was organized, with a pilot called Jack Knight due to take over one of the planes in Nebraska. Bonfires were lit to guide the flight and a relief pilot arranged, but the flight was so delayed that the bonfires had fizzled out, and his relief pilot had gone home. Knight took two mouthfuls of coffee and, with only some road maps to guide him, flew on in the dark, reaching Chicago at 8am. The mail was transferred and reached New York in a record time of 33 hours and 20 minutes. It would have taken 72 hours by train. The airmail service was secured.

COMFORT IN THE AIR

The Boeing Airplane Company was started by William Boeing in 1917. In 1933, the Boeing 247 became the first modern commercial aeroplane. It was all metal, low winged, and had twin engines. It was also the first airliner with retractable landing gear. With its soundproof, heated cabin and upholstered seats, its ten passengers travelled in unprecedented comfort.

THE AIRLINES OF EUROPE

Many countries were developing airlines in the 1930s. Various European airlines set about extending their routes to their colonies, offering scheduled services around the world.

PIONEERS OF THE AIR
-A Time Line-

~1927~
Charles Lindbergh flies solo across the Atlantic in 33½ hours

Kingsford-Smith and Ulm fly round Australia

~1928~
Amundsen reaches North Pole

Amelia Earhart crosses the Atlantic as a passenger

Kingsford-Smith and Ulm are the first to cross the Pacific

~1929~
Jimmy Doolittle makes the first instrument-controlled flight

~1930~
Amy Johnson flies solo to Australia

Frank Whittle files first patent for a jet engine

~1932~
Auguste Piccard ascends to a record height in a balloon

Amelia Earhart becomes the first woman to fly solo across the Atlantic

~1937~
The airship Hindenburg explodes as it tries to land in America

Imperial Airways inaugurates the first transatlantic air service

Germany develops the Messerschmitt fighter plane

Frank Whittle tests the jet engine

SCRAMBLE!

These two Canadian pilots are scrambling for take off in their Hurricanes during the Battle of Britain. Grabbing their helmets and parachutes, they were in the air within minutes. The Royal Canadian Air Force fought with the R.A.F. throughout the war. Canada participated in the Commonwealth Air Training Plan which trained 132,000 members of air crew.

THE MESSERSCHMITT BF 109 B

The Messerschmitt BF 109 played a significant part in the war. It was designed by Willy Messerschmitt, a young pilot who had learned his skills as a glider pilot. He was able to develop his talents with the encouragement of the German Air Ministry. The Messerschmitt first flew in 1937 and was active against the allies in the Battle of Britain. It is estimated that 35,000 Messerschmitt BF 109s were built. A few remain in service today.

BATTLE OF BRITAIN

The Battle of Britain is considered to be one of the greatest historic battles. For almost two months 740 British snd allied pilots fought 3,500 German Luftwaffe pilots over the skies of Britain. Most of the Messerschmitts' 109's fuel was used up reaching Britain and so were not able to continue the fight for as long as the allied pilots. Having lost the battle, the German superiority in the air had been destroyed. The chance of a quick victory over Britain had gone forever, and the fear of invasion faded.

ENOLA GAY

Most American aircrew named the aeroplanes in which they flew. The *Enola Gay* was the name given to the Boeing B29 Superfortress piloted by Colonel Paul Tibbets. It dropped the first atom bomb on Hiroshima, destroying the city and killing 100,000 people. Three days later, another atom bomb was dropped in Nagasaki, forcing the Japanese to surrender on 14 August 1945.

PEARL HARBOR

Although the two countries were not at war, Japanese dive bombers operating from six aircraft carriers, attacked and destroyed the American Pacific Fleet at anchor in Pearl Harbor on 7 December 1941. This brought America into the war. Aircraft carriers were not unknown in the First World War, but by the Second, they were a major part of air and sea warfare.

The Second World War

The Second World War saw rapid developments in aviation technology. Communication, navigation, radio and radar were all developed and improved during the war years, as was the design of the aircraft and the engines. German bombing raids in the First World War had shown that the aeroplane could be used as an instrument of total war. The Italians used bombing tactics against ground soldiers in Abyssinia (Ethiopia) in 1936. And in the Spanish Civil War of 1937-39 the most advanced fighter plane of the time – the German Messerschmitt BF 109 – made its debut, and was to have a significant effect in the Second World War. It was the first aeroplane to be used as an offensive weapon. The first British fighters to confront the German Messerschmitts were the Hurricanes and Spitfires, and the scene was set for the greatest air battle ever fought – the Battle of Britain. The Second World War firmly established the use of aircraft in warfare.

SPITFIRE

One of the most famous fighters ever built was the Spitfire. It was designed by R.J. Mitchell who had earned his reputation designing the record-breaking British Schneider seaplanes. Outnumbered by the Hurricane in the Battle of Britain, its superior performance was directed at the escorting Messerschmitts, allowing the Hurricanes to attack the German bombers.

NEVER HAS SO MUCH BEEN OWED BY SO MANY TO SO FEW

Winston Churchill recognized the importance of all the allied pilots who fought in the Battle of Britain. The Germans underestimated the determined spirit of the Spitfire and Hurricane pilots. Flying aces emerged, but the R.A.F. were reluctant to name them – all who flew were heroes. They were the first pilots to successfully fly modern planes in combat and safeguard their country.

THE AEROPLANE
COMES OF AGE

ENGINES TODAY

The Whittle turbojet became the forerunner of today's fast, modern engines.

The Second World War saw an acceleration in the innovation and development of aircraft. In six years, guided missiles and nuclear weapons had supplemented machine guns and high-explosive bombs; the piston engine was replaced by the gas turgine (turbo jets). The principle of the jet engine had been known for some time, and by the end of the Second World War it was being used on military planes by both sides. Plans were also being considered for the first commercial passenger jets. Speed became a new challenge. In 1924 the speed record was 447 kilometres (278 miles) per hour. By 1934 the speed record was 707 kilometres (440 miles) per hour. Charles (Chuck) Yeager broke the sound barrier in the Bell X-1, which was called *Glamorous Glennis* after his wife.

BREAKING THE SOUND BARRIER

Chuck Yeager, an American war veteran, was an outstanding test pilot of his time. On 14 October 1947, the Bell X-1 was lifted into the air by a mother plane – a B29 – to conserve fuel. On being released, Yeager opened up the four-chamber rocket engines for an all-out attempt to reach supersonic flight.

DE HAVILLAND'S COMET

De Havilland had always been an innovative company and, in 1949, the first pure jetliner, Comet 1, left Heathrow. In 1952 it began its first scheduled flights but was temporarily withdrawn from service two years later following a series of crashes. The cause was traced to fuselage fatigue problems which were overcome and some are still flying commercially today.

REFUELLING IN MID-AIR

Endurance and distance records, as well as transatlantic flights, prompted the technology of aerial refuelling. The Harrow Tanker provided the first service in 1939, and now it is common practice for jet fighters and some long-haul flights to refuel in mid-air.

THE JUMBO JET

In 1952 the first jetliner had 44 seats. By the 1970s wide-body jets were revolutionizing commercial air travel. The Boeing 747 was at the forefront of these new jet aircraft. With 350 seats or more, they were given the name Jumbo Jets.

FRANK WHITTLE
(1907-1996)

Like two other young engineers in Germany, Pabst von Obain and Werner von Braun, Frank Whittle knew that the principle of a jet engine was similar to rocket propulsion. Whilst the two Germans were developing their own ideas, Whittle was struggling to gain any encouragement from the British Air Ministry. In 1937, the first successful test run of his jet engine took place and the Air Ministry started to take an interest. But it was the Germans who developed the first jet aircraft in 1939 with the Heinkel HE 178. Two years later, Whittle's engine was tested on the Gloster E28/39.

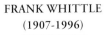

SUPERSONIC FLIGHT

There are many problems with supersonic flight. Air becomes so compressed that it forms solid shock waves. Shock waves occur when air flowing over any part of the aircraft reaches supersonic speed – 1,226 kilometres (760 miles) per hour at sea level, decreasing at heights to 1,061 kilometres (660 miles) per hour – or more simply Mach 1. There had been a number of attempts to break the sound barrier without success. Yeager had full confidence in his aircraft and when the needle on his Machmeter swung past Mach .94 on to .96 to .98, he felt the bucking and shuddering of the shock waves, then they suddenly stopped. He had reached Mach 1.05 (1,126 kilometres per hour) and the calmer conditions that lie beyond the sound barrier. He described it as an 'eerie quiet'.

WHITTLE ENGINE

In 1930, Sir Frank Whittle filed his first patent for a jet engine and, on 12 April 1937, his first turbojet had its maiden run. Following many experiments, Whittle could control and test the engine at speeds two or three times faster than a conventional piston engine.

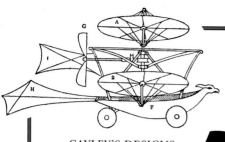

VERTICAL LIFT

CAYLEY'S DESIGNS

The principle of rotary movement lifting a weight upwards was well known. In 1843, Sir George Cayley designed this early helicopter, but it was never built.

*T*he best known Vertical Take Off and Landing (VTOL) aircraft is the helicopter. The principle of rotary movement lifting a weight upwards was well known. Both Leonardo da Vinci and Sir George Cayley had designed helicopters, but it was not until 400 years later that the first one was ever flown. After the Second World War, Igor Sikorsky designed a single rotor helicopter and pioneered helicopter trials in Russia. Helicopters have proved invaluable both for the military and the rescue services. Their advantage is that they can hover, take off, rise vertically, and land in a restricted space.

THE NATURAL ROTOR

The idea of rotor power can be seen in nature, as this sycamore seed pod demonstrates. This natural rotor may have provided the inspiration for early helicopter designs.

IGOR SIKORSKY (1889-1972)

Russian-born aviator, Igor Sikorsky, was the first man to solve the difficulties of 'torque' – the reason why earlier helicopter designs had been unsuccessful. The problem was that a machine rotating in one direction will produce a torque reaction in the other direction, so as the rotor blades of a helicopter turned in one direction, the helicopter itself turned in the other. Sikorsky controlled this torque reaction by fitting a small rotor on the tail. He produced the first successful practical helicopter the VS 300 in 1941 in America, when he hovered in the air for 102 minutes. Sikorsky helicopters are used today, based on his original revolutionary design.

HARRIER JUMP JET

The Hawker Siddeley Harrier is a VTOL (Vertical Take Off and Landing) aircraft. Representing significant advances in aircraft design, jet nozzles direct the exhaust downwards when taking off and landing.

THE FIRST FLIGHT

In 1907 Paul Cornu, a mechanic from France, became the first person to fly in a helicopter, hovering just off the ground for 20 seconds. However, the fuselage rotated in the opposite direction to the rotor blades causing him to crash to the ground. His delicate machine broke into many pieces.

THE FLYING BEDSTEAD

The first free-flight demonstration of direct jet lift was given by Rolls Royce in 1954. Their 'Flying Bedstead' successfully demonstrated manoeuvrability in free flight and provided invaluable information and research for the design of the first jump jet.

TO THE RESCUE

Even in the early days, the advantages of helicopters were recognized. Because helicopters can take off and land in a restricted space, and can hover in one place, they have become invaluable in everyday life. Landing on rooftops in busy cities is beneficial to business, but probably their most important role is as a rescue vehicle. They are used by the emergency services for air-sea rescues, mountain rescues and as air ambulances.

Today's Skies

hanks to the pioneers of the past there isn't a country today that cannot be reached by a jet airliner within 24 hours. Today's airports have to cope with the millions of passengers and aircraft that pass through them each year. Some 2,000 aeroplanes can take off from major airports in a day. A vast team of people are on hand to make sure that the planes land safely, are quickly turned round and sent off on their way again. Today, air travel is a popular and reasonably cheap form of transport. Airliners are larger, and more comfortable. Smaller jets (like the one here) are sold to private clients. The skies are controlled with sophisticated systems and international networking to make air travel safer than ever before.

FREQUENT FLIERS

It has taken less than a century since the first ever controlled flight in 1903 for air travel to become part of every day life. Most people rarely look up when a plane flies overhead and many of us think nothing of boarding a plane. At busy airports planes take off and land every few minutes.

12:00 ZUR
12:05 PARIS
12:15 MILAN
12:25 AMSTERDAM
12:40 BERLIN-TEGE
12:45 BRUSSELS
12:50 GENEVA
12:55 NICE

IT'S A SMALL WORLD

Looking back over the 20th century, we can see it, not only as a time when people conquered the air, but a time when the pioneers led us towards an understanding of the world. Air travel really has made the world a smaller place. People from all walks of life are prepared to fly, venturing further afield and going to remote places that a century before were just names on a map.

CONCORDE

Rather than countries competing against each other as they did in the original race for the skies, many countries are working together, haring ideas, research and costs. Concorde, one of the most striking planes of all time, was a joint achievement between France and Britain. A technological triumph, Concorde can cruise at twice the speed of sound, flying from London to New York in just three and a half hours. It can, however, carry only 100 passengers and many cities have banned it because of its sonic boom.

AIR TRAFFIC CONTROL

Early aviators relied on morse code for communication. Radio now provides reliable round-the-world networking, so that pilots can remain constantly in touch with the air traffic controllers. With radar and radio, air travel is one of the safest forms of travel that exists today.

RADAR (RADIO DIRECTION AND RANGE)

British research had shown that radio waves are reflected by metal objects as early as 1934. It was also discovered that strong, frequent waves could be detected by a suitable receiver. The first radars were large ground stations. Radar proved its worth during the Battle of Britain as German pilots could not understand how the British knew their movements in advance.

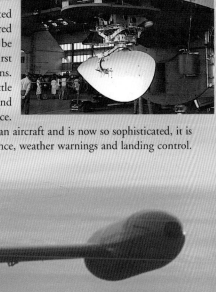

By 1941 radar was small enough to fit inside an aircraft and is now so sophisticated, it is involved with traffic control, collision avoidance, weather warnings and landing control.

The Pioneering Spirit

*T*he pioneering spirit still exists today. There are the adventurers who have set out to copy the record-breaking attempts of their predecessors. Louis Blériot, a Parisian solicitor, rebuilt one of his grandfather's aircraft and, in 1998, he attempted to repeat the historical journey of 1909. Unfortunately, on this occasion he was unsuccessful. At the present time, NASA is investigating the National Aerospace Plane, capable of flying at 10 times the speed of sound. There are new designs, new challenges, all of which contribute to keeping the spirit of adventure alive.

ROUND THE WORLD IN A BALLOON

When Auguste Piccard made his record-breaking, high-altitude flight in his balloon in 1932, he reached a height of 17,000 metres (56,000 feet). Today, the race is on to make aviation history and establish a new record – to fly non-stop around the world in a balloon.

FROM MYTH TO REALITY

In 1985 a team of engineers from the Massachusetts Institute of Technology in America set out to follow the mythical flight of Daedalus in the Greek story of Daedalus and Icarus. Their aim was to fly the 119 kilometres (74 miles) between the Greek islands of Crete and Santorini in a man-powered machine. Their machine was an aircraft with a wing span as wide as a Boeing 727, but it weighed only 32 kilogrammes (70lbs). It was named *Daedalus* and was powered by Kanellos Kanellopoulos, a Greek bicycle champion – who was chosen for his amazing endurance. In April 1998, Kanellopoulos pedalled the distance in four hours, splashing down safely just short of land – and set a new world record for human-powered flight.

HOTOL

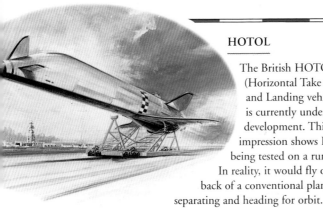

The British HOTOL (Horizontal Take Off and Landing vehicle) is currently under development. This artist's impression shows HOTOL being tested on a runway. In reality, it would fly on the back of a conventional plane before separating and heading for orbit.

PIONEERS OF THE AIR
-A TIME LINE-

~1939~

First transatlantic mail service begins

The Heinkel HE 178 becomes the first jet-powered aircraft

~1940~

Battle of Britain takes place

~1941~

Igor Sikorsky designs a single rotor helicopter

Gloster E28/39 is tested

~1945~

Atomic bomb dropped on Hiroshima

~1947~

Chuck Yeager breaks sound barrier

~1949~

The first jet-engine liner, Comet 1, is unveiled

~1954~

Rolls Royce demonstrate the first direct jet lift with their Flying Bedstead

~1986~

Dick Rutan and Jeana Yeager fly non-stop around world without refuelling

~1998~

The Daedalus project sets the record for the longest man-powered flight.

VOYAGER

In 1986, a new long-distance aviation record was set when Dick Rutan and Jeana Yeager flew non-stop around the world without refuelling. This took them just nine days in their aircraft, *Voyager*. When they landed, they had just 37 gallons of fuel left in the tanks which had contained 1,200 gallons on take-off.

STEALTH BOMBER

Military aeroplanes have developed in speed and performance due to the development of the jet engine. The American Lockheed F-117A Stealth Fighter is designed to be undetectable by enemy radar. Its surfaces are faceted which enables it to deflect radar signals.

FLIGHT OF THE FUTURE?

A passenger plane that flies at hypersonic speed on the edges of space may appear in the near future. NASA is investigating the National Aerospace Plane (right), which could fly at 6,500 miles an hour –10 times the speed of sound.

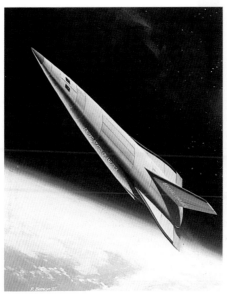

DID YOU KNOW?

Marco Polo started his journey from China to Portugal in 1275. It took five years. Today, that same journey by aeroplane takes five hours.

The Wright Brothers named their plane the *Flyer* after the most successful bicycle they had built in their workshops.

W. W. Balantyne is reputed to have been the first aerial stowaway. He was a crew member of the R34 airship, but was taken off at the last minute to lighten the load. Determined to be on the ship as it attempted to cross the Atlantic, he hid in the rigging between two gas bags. Unfortunately, breathing in the hydrogen made him sick and he had to give himself up. He was then made to work his passage for the rest of the journey. A second stowaway, the ship's cat called Wopsie, was also found. They were both feted when the airship finally landed in America.

The Flying Fraulein was a young German woman called Hanna Reisch who received an Iron Cross from Hitler. Her first love was gliding and she could manage the gliders as well as, if not better, than her male counterparts. She became a test pilot on both planes and helicopters, and became the first woman in Germany to be given airforce rank.

The Anatov, An225 is the heaviest aircraft ever to fly. It has a 40 metre (130 foot) long cargo-hold and each of its six engines delivers a 54,000 lb thrust.

The F.A. Cup Final in 1930 between Arsenal and Huddersfield had to be stopped for 20 minutes while the *Graf Zeppelin* flew overhead.

Alan Cobham set off to fly to Australia from England in 1926. A sandstorm forced him to fly low over Iraq and Bedouin tribesman, who had never seen an aeroplane before, tried to shoot it down. Unfortunately a bullet hit the co-pilot who later died in hospital.

Galbraith Rodgers set off to fly from New York to California in a Baby Wright plane in 1911. The journey took 50 days and he made 69 stops, 16 of which were crash landings. Wherever he stopped, people rushed to take souvenirs from the plane, so it was fortunate that the ground crew had plenty of spare parts. When he finally reached California, only two pieces of the original plane were left.

ACKNOWLEDGEMENTS

The publishers would like to thank: Graham Rich, Hazel Poole and Elizabeth Wiggans for their assistance and David Hobbs for his map of the world.
Copyright © 1998 ticktock Publishing Ltd.
First published in Great Britain by ticktock Publishing Ltd, The Offices in the Square, Hadlow, Tonbridge, Kent, TN11 0DD. All rights reserved.
No part of this publication may be reproduced, stored in a retrieval system, or transmitted in any form or by any means electronic, mechanical, photocopying, recording or otherwise, without prior written permission of the copyright owner.
A CIP catalogue record for this book is available from the British Library. ISBN 1 86007 078 7
Picture research by Image Select.
Printed in Great Britain.

Picture Credits: t=top, b=bottom, c=centre, l=left, r=right, OFC=outside front cover, OBC=outside back cover, IFC=inside front cover

AKG; 9br, 15br, 17cb, 21tr. Ann Ronan; 3br & OFC. Ann Ronan @ Image Select; 2/3b, 8cb, 8/9t, 10bl, 14tl, 27bl & OFC. Aviation Photographs International; OFC (main pic), 13br, 14/15b, 15cr, 16/17ct, 16/17cb, 20/21c, 22/23c, 23tr, 29cr, 31cr, 30/31c & OFC. C.M.Scott; 16bl, 27c. Colorific!; 22cl. Corbis-Bettmann; 24bl. Gamma; 30br. Giraudon; 2bl, 5cr, 6tl, 13c, 14/15t & OBC, 13c. Greg Evans International Photo Library; 2tl, 6tl. Hulton Deutsch Collection Ltd; 7tr, 23br. Hulton Getty; 14bl, 19tr, 22tl, 26tr, 27cr. Image Select; 8/9b & OFC, 17br & OFC, 22bl, 24br, 25c. Mary Evans Picture Library; 3c, 5tr, 10tl, 11tl, 20bl. Philip Jarrett; 4tl, 6bl, 7bl, 6bl, 7bl. PIX; 2/3t, 4bl, 5br, 6/7t, 12bl, 27br, 28bl, 28/29 (main pic), 29tr. Planet Earth Pictures/Space Frontiers; 31br. Quadrant Picture Library; IFC, 11ct, 10/11c, 12/13c & 32ct, 13t, 24/25c, 24/25t, 25tr, 25br, 24/25c & OFC, 26bl, 28tl, 31tl. Retrograph Archive Ltd; 20bl, 21br, 21br. Salamander Picture Library; 22/23b. Science and Society Picture Library; 4/5 & OFC. Science Photo Library; 26c. Sutton Libraries and Art Services; 16tl. The Breitling Company; 30tl. Telegraph Colour Library; 24/25ct & OFC, 26/27t & OBC, 29cl. The Smithsonian Institution; 6/7c & OBC, 7cr, 9tr, 9cr, 10/11c & OFC, 10/11b, 12tl, 18/19c. The Advertising Archive; 20tl. UPI/Corbis; 19bl, 20/21t, 21bl.

Every effort has been made to trace the copyright holders and we apologize in advance for any unintentional omissions.
We would be pleased to insert the appropriate acknowledgement in any subsequent edition of this publication.

snapping-turtle
guide

SCHOOLS LIBRARY SERVICE